How To Use This Study Guide

This five-lesson study guide corresponds to *"How To Open the Window of Heaven Over Your Life" With Rick Renner* (Renner TV). Each lesson in this study guide covers a topic that is addressed during the program series, with questions and references supplied to draw you deeper into your own private study of the Scriptures on this subject.

To derive the most benefit from this study guide, consider the following:

First, watch or listen to the program prior to working through the corresponding lesson in this guide. (Programs can also be viewed at **renner.org** by clicking on the Media/Archive links.)

Second, take the time to look up the scriptures included in each lesson. Prayerfully consider their application to your own life.

Third, use a journal or notebook to make note of your answers to each lesson's Study Questions and Practical Application challenges.

Fourth, invest specific time in prayer and in the Word of God to consult with the Holy Spirit. Write down the scriptures or insights He reveals to you.

Finally, take action! Whatever the Lord tells you to do according to His Word, do it.

For added insights on this subject, it is recommended that you obtain Rick Renner's book *A Life Ablaze*. You may also select from Rick's other available resources by placing your order at **renner.org** or by calling 1-800-742-5593.

LESSON 1

TOPIC

God Is Generous With the Generous

SCRIPTURES

1. **Matthew 6:21** — For where your treasure is, there will your heart be also.
2. **Galatians 6:7** — Be not deceived; God is not mocked: for whatsoever a man soweth, that shall he also reap.
3. **Acts 10:38** — How God anointed Jesus of Nazareth with the Holy Ghost and with power: who went about doing good, and healing all that were oppressed of the devil; for God was with him.
4. **Acts 2:44,45** — And all that believed were together, and had all things in common; and sold their possessions and goods, and parted them to all men, as every man had need.
5. **Luke 6:38** (*NLT*) — …Your gift will return to you in full — pressed down, shaken together to make room for more, running over, and poured into your lap. The amount you give will determine the amount you get back.
6. **2 Corinthians 9:6** — …He which soweth sparingly shall reap also sparingly; and he which soweth bountifully shall reap also bountifully.
7. **Proverbs 11:24,25** (*ESV*) — One gives freely, yet grows all the richer; another withholds what he should give, and only suffers want. Whoever brings blessing will be enriched, and one who waters will himself be watered.
8. **Proverbs 22:9** (*ESV*) — Whoever has a bountiful eye will be blessed….
9. **Psalm 112:5** (*NIV*) — Good will come to those who are generous….

GREEK WORDS

1. "where" — ὅπου (*hopou*): exactly where; in the place
2. "treasure" — θησαυρός (*thsauros*): a treasure; money, riches, or investments
3. "there" — ἐκεῖ (*ekei*): there; exactly there

SYNOPSIS

The five lessons in this study on *How To Open the Window of Heaven Over Your Life* will focus on the following topics:

- God Is Generous With the Generous
- How God Responds to Sacrificial Giving
- How To Open the Window of Heaven Over Your Life
- What Jesus Said About Giving
- What the Apostle Paul Said About Giving

The emphasis of this lesson:

What we do with our money — how we spend it, save it, and give it — reveals a great deal about our priorities in life and tells the real story of how much we are in love with God. It also determines how blessed we're going to be. It is imperative for us to understand what God has to say about giving so we can learn how to become generous and open the window of heaven over our lives.

Money is often not a subject people like talking about, especially in the context of ministry or church. But the truth is, people talk to us about money all the time no matter where we are.

For example, when you go to the grocery store, you walk the aisles, packing your cart full of groceries. But then before you leave, they stop you at the register and ask you for money. The same thing happens when you go to a movie. You excitedly walk up to the counter, but before they will give you a ticket, the cashier asks you for money. What about when you go out to eat? After eating a delicious meal and perhaps enjoying warm company, what happens next? The waiter hands you the bill and asks you for money.

Everywhere we go, people talk to us about money, so why does it surprise us that God addresses the issue of money? In fact, this subject is so important that Jesus discussed it more than any other topic in Scripture.

The Great Revealer of Our Heart

In Matthew 6:21, Jesus makes a remarkable statement about money:

> **For where your treasure is, there will your heart be also.**

The word "where" in Greek means *exactly where* or *in that very place*. It could be translated, "*Exactly* where your treasure is…" or, "*In the very place* where your treasure is…." The word "treasure" is the Greek word *thsauros*, and it describes *a treasure, money, riches*, or *investments*.

This verse tells us that in *the very place* where your money is — where your *investments* and *resources* are — there will be your heart also. The word "there" in Greek is the word *ekei*, which means *exactly there*. Jesus is clearly and simply teaching that money tells the story of where our heart is.

Money is the great revealer of what is inside our heart, and what we do with our money reveals how much we really love the Lord and the work of the ministry.

One person put it this way, "You can give without loving, but you cannot love without giving." That's because when you love someone, you usually want to invest in them or do something sacrificial for them. Why do we do that? **Because that is where our heart is, and our money follows our heart.**

If a person really loves the Lord and loves the work of the ministry, he's going to put his treasure into the ministry, or into the church, because that is where his heart is. If you want to know where *your* heart is, follow your money and you'll find out — because money really does tell the truth.

Rick's Personal Testimony

Rick shared that when he was young, he was a terrible giver. He was afraid to give and did not have faith to believe for finances. Although Rick grew up in a wonderful home, giving was a very tense issue for their family, and as a result Rick was never really taught to give.

After Rick and Denise were married, they joined a large Baptist church as associate pastors, and their lead pastor began preaching on Galatians 6:7, which says, "Be not deceived; God is not mocked: for whatsoever a man soweth, that shall he also reap." He preached on the same verse week after week, trying to drive the revelation of giving and receiving into the hearts of all the church members.

At the time, Rick was not giving, and he would get embarrassed when Denise asked him, "Rick, are we giving?" Rick would even try to deflect her question, saying, "Denise, how could you even ask me such a question?" Because the truth was, Rick was not giving.

Eventually, Rick decided that if he wanted to have a blessed life, he needed to learn how to be generous. Do you know why? Because **God is generous with the generous.**

That is the secret of giving. It is not a burden to give — it is a *blessing*. When you are generous, it opens the window of Heaven over your life for God to be financially generous with you.

God's Example of Generosity

God Himself is our greatest example of generosity. When it was time for God to give to the world, He gave the very best of what He had — He gave His Son Jesus. And think about how generous God is with you today. He's generous in the mercy He gives you. He's generous in the love He shows you. He's generous in patience and forgiveness — everything about God is generous.

Jesus was, and is, generous too. He even passed that generosity on to His apostles, and they passed it on to the Early Church. Notice in the following verse how generous Jesus was:

> How God anointed Jesus of Nazareth with the Holy Ghost and with power: who went about doing good, and healing all that were oppressed of the devil; for God was with him.
> —**Acts 10:38**

Most people who read this verse assume "doing good" refers to Jesus healing and casting out demons, but when you read this in the Greek, you see that the words "doing good" can only be translated one way. It is the Greek word for *a philanthropist, one who financially supports charitable works,* or *a person who uses his financial resources to meet the needs of disadvantaged people.*

Jesus had finances and resources that were available to Him, and this verse tells us that a large part of Jesus' ministry was to use those resources to meet other people's needs. Jesus not only healed the sick, cast out demons, and preached the Word of God, He also generously reached out to help those who were disadvantaged.

Hebrews 13:8 tells us, "Jesus Christ is the same yesterday, and to day, and for ever." Since Jesus was generous then, He is still generous now. What He did then, He is still doing now. And since Jesus is generous, we need to be generous too.

Generosity Flowed in the Early Church

In Acts 2:44 and 45, we read about the generosity of the Early Church:

> **And all that believed were together, and had all things in common; and sold their possessions and goods, and parted them to all men, as every man had need.**

After the Day of Pentecost, the Early Church became spiritually alive. They had been touched by the power of God on that day, and as a result, they opened their hearts to God and began to share what they had. They generously gave and sold their possessions in order to meet each other's needs.

When God touched these believers' hearts, they said, "Lord, what we have is Yours!" They were not stingy; they gave generously. As they continued to be generous with God and with each other, God became generous with *them*, and signs and wonders erupted in their midst!

It is often a sign that God has moved in a person's heart when they begin to open their wallet or purse and say, "Lord, everything I have is Yours." That's because open hearts are *generous*. And that's exactly what happened in the Early Church.

From Stingy to Generous

As we saw previously, when Rick and Denise were first married, the pastor at their church began to preach from Galatians 6:7: "Be not deceived; God is not mocked: for whatsoever a man soweth, that shall he also reap."

The church at that time was very old and traditional, and the people were pretty stingy in their giving. That's why the pastor was preaching on Galatians 6:7. He wasn't after people's money — he wanted them to be blessed. He knew that if they would be generous with God, God would respond generously to them.

Eventually, one man in the congregation received this revelation about giving and receiving, and he gave a huge, sacrificial gift. The next week the pastor announced the gift that was given to the rest of the church, and suddenly God began to move upon their hearts. Week by week, Rick and Denise watched this old, stingy congregation become extremely generous with God.

As people opened their wallets to God, it was like God said, "I really like what's going on there. I'm going to come down now and be generous with them," and the power of the Holy Spirit poured out on that old, traditional church.

Miracles began to happen, and the altar was filled with people coming forward to give their lives to Christ. God showed up and became generous with them because of their generous giving.

You Reap What You Sow

When you open your heart — and wallet — to God, it puts you in a position for God to pour out His generosity on you. And the more you give, the more that comes back to you because God is the greatest giver in the universe, and He won't let you outgive Him.

Jesus affirms this in Luke 6:38, "…Your gift will return to you in full — pressed down, shaken together to make room for more, running over, and poured into your lap. The amount you give will determine the amount you get back" (*NLT*).

If you're generous with God, He is going to show you how generous He can be with you. Although, we find in Scripture that the opposite is also true. If you're stingy with your giving, what comes back to you may be dramatically less.

> **…He which soweth sparingly shall reap also sparingly; and he which soweth bountifully shall reap also bountifully.**
> **— 2 Corinthians 9:6**

If you give little, you're going to reap little. But if you sow generously, you'll reap generously. That is exactly what Second Corinthians 9:6 says. It couldn't be any clearer. If we're stingy, we're going to experience stingy results, but if we're generous, we're going to experience the generous supply of Heaven.

Take the Dead Sea as an example. There is nothing living in the Dead Sea. Do you know why? It has no outlet, so it is just a receiver. Although the Jordan River is filled with fish and all kinds of life, after the water flows into the Dead Sea it becomes dead. The Dead Sea continually receives from the Jordan River, but because it has no outlet, it does not have the ability to produce or sustain life.

Interestingly, scientists say that if an outlet could be provided for the Dead Sea and water could flow out, then the waters of the Dead Sea would come alive. This is a powerful example to believers of what God does *not* want us to be.

God never intended for Christians to be on the receiving side only, taking money and possessions and keeping them to ourselves. God intends for what we receive to flow right through us. As we have generously received, we need to generously give. And as long as we're giving generously, we'll remain spiritually vital and vibrant. That is the truth!

When Christians only invest in themselves and their own family and friends, they are not operating as God intended. God made us to be generous with others just like He is with us, and as we are faithful to do that, we can rest assured that no matter how generous we are, we'll never outgive God.

Generosity Starts With the Heart

How do you know if you are a generous person? When a person does something generous, it is because he or she has a generous attitude. Generous people are not thinking about how little they can give; they're thinking, "Oh, I wish I could have done more." The attitude of their heart is to be generous.

Generosity is not just about what you give to the ministry, what you give to the Lord, or what you give to the church. Generosity is demonstrated by what kind of tip you leave in a restaurant, what kind of tip you leave for the person who cuts or colors your hair, or what kind of tip you leave for the person who works on your car. Generosity is not just an action — it is an attitude that flows freely from the heart.

If you were to ask God today, "God, am I generous or am I stingy?" how would He answer you? It's important to ask this question because God is generous with the generous. And if you want God to be generous with you, you need to become a generous person.

Look at what the Bible says about those who are generous:

> **One gives freely, yet grows all the richer; another withholds what he should give, and only suffers want. Whoever brings**

blessing will be enriched, and one who waters will himself be watered.
— **Proverbs 11:24,25 (*ESV*)**

This clearly says that what we do to others will happen to us. Proverbs 22:9 also tells us, "Whoever has a bountiful eye will be blessed…" (*ESV*). When we're generous, we start to see things differently. We begin to look for opportunities to be a blessing to other people. And Psalm 112:5 literally tells us that God will come to those who are generous.

Being generous opens up the window of heaven over our lives. When we are generous, God promises to come and be generous with us too. As we are obedient to give, we will live blessed lives.

STUDY QUESTIONS

Study to shew thyself approved unto God, a workman that needeth not to be ashamed, rightly dividing the word of truth.
— **2 Timothy 2:15**

1. What does Luke 12:32-34 say to do? What does this passage tell us about God's attitude toward us?
2. What does Second Corinthians 9:7 and 8 tell us about the kind of giver we should be?
3. Acts 2:42-47 tells us what the Early Church was like after Pentecost. We know that they gave and sold their possessions to help one another (*see* vv. 44,45). What else does this passage say the Early Church did?

PRACTICAL APPLICATION

But be ye doers of the word, and not hearers only, deceiving your own selves.
— **James 1:22**

1. Jesus said in Matthew 6:21 that where you put your "treasure" reveals where your heart is. What are the treasures in your life? Write down two or three places your money and resources go and reflect on what that reveals about your heart.
2. Maybe, like Rick, you were never taught to give. What are three things you've learned about giving and generosity in this lesson?

3. What is an area of your life that you could be more generous in? If you're not sure, pray and ask the Holy Spirit where to start.

LESSON 2

TOPIC

How God Responds to Sacrificial Giving

SCRIPTURES

1. **Matthew 6:21** — For where your treasure is, there will your heart be also.
2. **2 Samuel 24:22** — ...Let my lord the king take and offer up what seemeth good unto him; behold, here be oxen for burnt sacrifice, and threshing instruments and other instruments of the oxen for wood.
3. **2 Samuel 24:24** — ...Neither will I offer burnt offerings unto the Lord my God of that which doth cost me nothing....
4. **2 Samuel 24:24,25** — ...David bought the threshingfloor and the oxen for fifty shekels of silver. And David built there an altar unto the Lord, and offered burnt offerings and peace offerings....
5. **2 Chronicles 1:6** — And Solomon went up thither to the brasen altar before the Lord, which was at the tabernacle of the congregation, and offered a thousand burnt offerings upon it.
6. **2 Chronicles 1:7** (*NIV*) — That night God appeared to Solomon and said to him, "Ask for whatever you want me to give you."
7. **2 Chronicles 7:1** — ...The fire came down from heaven, and consumed the burnt offering and the sacrifices; and the glory of the Lord filled the house.
8. **2 Chronicles 7:5** — And king Solomon offered a sacrifice of twenty and two thousand oxen, and an hundred and twenty thousand sheep: so the king and all the people dedicated the house of God.
9. **2 Chronicles 7:12** — And the Lord appeared to Solomon by night, and said unto him, I have heard thy prayer, and have chosen this place to myself for an house of sacrifice.

10. **Proverbs 3:9,10** — Honour the Lord with thy substance, and with the firstfruits of all thine increase: so shall thy barns be filled with plenty, and thy presses shall burst out with new wine.

GREEK WORDS
1. "where" — ὅπου (*hopou*): exactly where; in the place
2. "treasure" — θησαυρός (*thsauros*): a treasure; money, riches, or investments
3. "there" — ἐκεῖ (*ekei*): there; exactly there

SYNOPSIS
Our giving opens up the window of Heaven, allowing God's generosity to flow into our life. In the previous lesson, we saw how God is generous with those who are generous and that being generous actually frees us to live a blessed life.

We can find out whether we are generous or not by looking at where our money goes (*see* Matthew 6:21). If we are generous like God, our money will go to meet the needs of others and sow into His Kingdom. If we are stingy, we will keep our money and resources to ourselves. It's important for us to learn to be generous because God was first generous with us when He gave the very best He had — His Son Jesus.

We are meant to be generous just as God is generous, and as we willingly give, God promises to meet our needs abundantly (*see* Luke 6:38). The more we give or sow, the more we will reap His blessings in our lives.

The emphasis of this lesson:

When we give sacrificially and ask God to show up, He responds generously by showing up in our lives in remarkable ways. Sacrificial giving involves giving God our heart and mind and everything we have in a way that costs us something. And as we do, God will respond to our need supernaturally.

In the last lesson, we looked at Matthew 6:21, which says, "For where your treasure is, there will your heart be also."

The word "where" in Greek means *exactly where, in the very place*, and the word "treasure" is the Greek word *thsauros*, meaning *a treasure, money, riches*, or *investments*. The word "there" is also the Greek word *ekei*, meaning *there* or *exactly there*. Jesus was teaching that *in the very place* you put your money, *exactly there* will your heart be also, because where we put our money reveals what is in our heart.

When you love somebody, you want to give to that person and invest in him or her because you believe in that individual. In the same way, when you love God and His Kingdom, you'll want to give to Him because your money will follow your heart. And we have this promise from Scripture — when we are generous with God, He will be generous with us.

A Sacrificial Gift

The Old Testament is filled with examples of sacrificial giving. When people decided to bring a sacrificial gift to God in ancient times, they had to plan and think ahead to make it happen. They couldn't just bring a gift — God required them to build an altar first. In fact, God even gave specific instructions for how altars needed to be built.

For example, certain kinds of stones had to be chosen and then those stones had to be cleaned and arranged properly. The place where the altar was going to be built had to be ceremonially cleansed too. After the altar was prepared, wood had to be gathered and placed on top of the altar, and the very best animal had to be chosen from the flock for the sacrifice. That means whoever was offering the sacrifice had to go through his entire flock to look for the animal that had no defects and was better than all the other animals.

This was not an event that happened on a whim. A lot of planning and forethought went into deciding and preparing to bring a sacrificial gift. Sometimes it took two weeks and sometimes it took a year to get everything ready to bring a sacrificial offering to God. And that's the way God designed it because He sees the entire event, including the planning and preparation, as part of the sacrifice.

Your intention, your desire, your preparation — everything you have to do to pull the money together to give — all of it in addition to the gift itself is considered part of your sacrificial gift to God.

Historically when people offered sacrificial gifts to God, they also took that opportunity to call upon the name of the Lord and offer their petition. As their offering burned on the altar, they would stand in front of the altar and say to God, "This is what I ask you to do." And, if people needed God to be extra generous with them, they would bring a very generous offering. Even back then, people understood that God responds generously to those who are generous with Him.

The Pattern of the Patriarchs

In the Old Testament, we find that from the very beginning of time, the patriarchs of our faith built altars at very critical moments in their lives. One example of this is Noah, who was the first person recorded in the Bible to build an altar.

When the ark finally rested on the mountains of Ararat and Noah stepped out to see the whole world was a big, muddy mess, Noah probably knew he needed divine assistance. So what did he do? He built an altar in order to offer a sacrifice.

Noah, probably with the help of his sons, would have had to collect the proper stones as God required and arrange them correctly. Imagine, all the time they spent collecting stones they were probably thinking about what they were doing. They were preparing to make a sacrifice.

As Noah and his sons arranged the stones carefully, according to God's specifications, they were thinking about the sacrifice they were going to make. When they gathered the wood to place on top of the altar and when they sorted through all the animals to find the very best one to offer to God, they were thinking about the sacrifice.

When the burnt offering was finally made and smoke was billowing into the air, the Bible tells us the Lord was pleased and He responded to Noah (*see* Genesis 8:21). Noah gave generously and called on the name of the Lord, and God responded generously to Noah.

Another example is found in Genesis 12 when Abraham, Sarah, and Lot came into the land of promise. When they arrived, they found giants everywhere! How did Abraham respond? He built an altar.

Probably with the help of Lot, Abraham began gathering stones just as Noah did, cleansing and arranging the stones according to God's specifications. Then he searched for the very best animal that he could bring to God. Nothing about it was accidental. The entire process was very intentional. And in response to his gift, God protected Abraham and generously provided for him.

Later when God brought Abraham out of Egypt, Abraham returned to the same spot where he had built his first altar, and he made another sacrifice. There he called upon the name of the Lord (*see* Genesis 13). And because Abraham gave generously, God generously responded to him.

We see again and again in Scripture that at critical junctures in Abraham's life — when he really felt a need for God's generous support — he built an altar and offered a generous sacrifice.

Another powerful example of this is found in Second Samuel 24, where we read about King David. A plague was ravaging Israel and had killed 70,000 people, so David wanted to offer a sacrifice to the Lord in order to bring an end to it.

David found the place where he wanted to build an altar but discovered the land was owned by a Jebusite. When the Jebusite learned David wanted to buy the land and offer a sacrifice, he basically said to David, "I'll give you the land, the wood, the stones — I'll even give you the animals to sacrifice. Take whatever you need from me." But listen to David's response in verse 24:

> **…Neither will I offer burnt offerings unto the Lord my God of that which doth cost me nothing.…**
> — **2 Samuel 24:24**

It was very kind of the Jebusite to offer, but David understood that it would not be a sacrifice if it did not cost him something. The passage goes on to say:

> **…David bought the threshingfloor and the oxen for fifty shekels of silver. And David built there an altar unto the Lord, and offered burnt offerings and peace offerings.…**
> — **2 Samuel 24:24,25**

God responded to David's generous sacrifice and the plague miraculously came to an end. God was so blessed by what David did that the piece of land David used eventually became the place where the temple was built in the city of Jerusalem.

These verses in Second Samuel 24 tell us something very significant about the attitude we need to have when we bring a sacrifice to God. In verse 24, David said it needed to cost him something. And if we want to give a real sacrifice, it needs to cost us something too. We need to give of our money, we need to give of our resources, and we need to give of our other kinds of gifts.

But the truth is, God doesn't need our money, resources, or gifts because God has it all. The cattle on a thousand hills belong to Him (*see* Psalm 50:10). The streets of Heaven are paved with gold. Every gate in Heaven is a massive pearl. And Heaven is filled with precious gems. God doesn't need our money, resources, or gifts; He wants our hearts. Jesus clearly said this in Matthew 6:21, "For where your treasure is, there will your heart be also."

God is not after our money; He is after our heart. And God knows that when we put our treasure into the Kingdom of God, our heart goes there. God is after our hearts.

Sacrificial Giving and God's Response

Scripture also shows us the greater the sacrifice we give to God, the greater the response from God. Another illustration of this is found in Second Chronicles 1:6, where Solomon had become the king of Israel after the passing of his father David.

Solomon was so overwhelmed by the responsibilities of being king that he decided to ask God for help. He had watched his father, David, give sacrifices before, so he knew what to do. The Bible tells us:

> **And Solomon went up thither to the brasen altar before the Lord, which was at the tabernacle of the congregation, and offered a thousand burnt offerings upon it.**
> **— 2 Chronicles 1:6**

In a single day, Solomon offered 1,000 burnt offerings to God. This was the biggest offering that had ever been offered in history to God in a single day. But to achieve such an undertaking in a single day, Solomon had to plan weeks, possibly even months, in advance.

The very best animals had to be selected, not just from Jerusalem but from all over the land of Israel. Then all the animals had to be transported to the city of Jerusalem, meaning corrals had to be built to hold them once they arrived. Then all the animals had to be cleansed, and, finally, they all had to be killed.

To pull all this off from beginning to end would have required thousands of workers. For Solomon to offer so many sacrifices in a single day, he had to invest a great deal of thought, time, and money. And all of this was done so that he could call upon the name of the Lord. He wanted to be generous because he needed a generous response from God.

How did God respond? Let's take a look at Second Chronicles 1:7, which says, "That night God appeared to Solomon and said to him, 'Ask for whatever you want me to give you'" (*NIV*).

God was so touched by Solomon's thoughtful, well-planned, generous giving that God wasted no time in responding. He showed up to Solomon that night, essentially saying, "Wow, nobody's ever given anything like this to Me before, so please tell Me what you want. Ask anything and I'll do it." That is a pretty generous response!

In Second Chronicles 7, the Bible tells us that Solomon made another sacrifice. Remembering what happened the first time when he gave 1,000 burnt offerings, Solomon said, "I wonder what would happen if I give even more?"

Second Chronicles 7:5 tells us:

> **And king Solomon offered a sacrifice of twenty and two thousand oxen, and an hundred and twenty thousand sheep: so the king and all the people dedicated the house of God.**

In a single day, Solomon sacrificed 22,000 oxen and 120,000 sheep. That amount is nearly unimaginable.

In the program, Rick shared about having lunch one day with a man who owned a large farm and a huge slaughterhouse, one of the biggest slaughterhouses in the United States. This man told Rick about the new technology they were able to use to slaughter cattle much faster.

Eventually this verse from Second Chronicles 7 came up, and as they discussed it, the man looked at Rick and said, "That is an amazing verse because even today with all the technology we have it would be impossible for us to slaughter 22,000 oxen and 120,000 sheep in a single day." He said for Solomon to do that would have required months and months of planning and thousands of workers. It was a huge event that had to be orchestrated and thought through well. But God saw that whole process from beginning to end as part of Solomon's sacrifice to Him.

Solomon's sacrifice was not a last-minute event. It required careful planning and an enormous amount of time, energy, labor, and organization for him to bring that kind of sacrifice to the Lord. Solomon's sacrifice was truly an extravagant expression of his heart.

And how did God respond this time? Second Chronicles 7:12 tells us:

> **And the Lord appeared to Solomon by night, and said unto him, I have heard thy prayer, and have chosen this place to myself for an house of sacrifice.**

That night God showed up again. Would you like God to show up in your life and ask you what you'd like Him to do for you? Then give something sacrificial; that's what Solomon did. He had learned the first time that God would show up, so he did the same thing again. But the second time Solomon was even more generous.

That is why Solomon wrote with great conviction the words in Proverbs 3:9 and 10:

> **Honour the Lord with thy substance, and with the firstfruits of all thine increase: so shall thy barns be filled with plenty, and thy presses shall burst out with new wine.**

This was coming from a man who had been generous with God. Solomon built an altar very intentionally, he offered something that really cost him something, and when he was offering his sacrifice, he called upon the name of the Lord. Then God showed up and responded generously to him.

Solomon knew that if he really honored God with what he had, God would move mightily on his behalf. And in the same way, if we need God to do something special in our life, we may need to do something sacrificial because, as we've seen in each of these examples, a blessing always comes with an extra, especially given, sacrificial gift.

Solomon discovered the principle of giving a sacrificial gift: when we honor God, He honors us, and when we're generous with God, He is amazingly generous with us.

STUDY QUESTIONS

> Study to shew thyself approved unto God, a workman that needeth not to be ashamed, rightly dividing the word of truth.
> — 2 Timothy 2:15

1. Why was God so blessed by David's sacrifice in Second Samuel 24? What happened as a result of David's sacrificial gift?
2. Read Psalm 33:13-22. If God already has everything He needs, why do we still need to bring sacrificial gifts to Him? What is it that God desires from us?
3. When God responded to Solomon in Second Chronicles 1:7-12, what does God say about Solomon's heart? What else did God give him besides wisdom?

PRACTICAL APPLICATION

> But be ye doers of the word, and not hearers only, deceiving your own selves.
> — James 1:22

1. What do you typically do to prepare an offering before you give it? List two or three things you do beforehand to plan and prepare to give a financial gift.
2. Can you imagine the number of animals, people, and tools that were involved in pulling off Solomon's second sacrifice in Second Chronicles 7:5? It was a truly incredible feat. Maybe you don't have thousands of cattle and sheep, but you do have something. What would it look like for you to prepare and give a sacrificial gift to the Lord?
3. Think about the impact David's generous giving had on Solomon when he became king. What could you pass on or teach to your children or grandchildren about the power of giving? Write down some ideas that come to mind.

LESSON 3

TOPIC
How To Open the Window of Heaven Over Your Life

SCRIPTURES
1. **Matthew 6:21** — For where your treasure is, there will your heart be also.
2. **Malachi 1:7-8** — Ye offer polluted bread upon mine altar; and ye say, Wherein have we polluted thee? In that ye say, The table of the Lord is contemptible. And if ye offer the blind for sacrifice, is it not evil? and if ye offer the lame and sick, is it not evil? offer it now unto thy governor; will he be pleased with thee, or accept thy person? saith the Lord of hosts.
3. **Malachi 1:10** — Who is there even among you that would shut the doors for nought? Neither do ye kindle fire on mine altar for nought. I have no pleasure in you, saith the Lord of hosts, neither will I accept an offering at your hand.
4. **Malachi 1:12** — But ye have profaned it, in that ye say, The table of the Lord is polluted; and the fruit thereof, even his meat, is contemptible.
5. **Malachi 1:13** — Ye said also, Behold, what a weariness is it! and ye have snuffed at it, saith the Lord of hosts; and ye brought that which was torn, and the lame, and the sick; thus ye brought an offering: should I accept this of your hand? saith the Lord.
6. **Malachi 3:7,8** — Even from the days of your fathers ye are gone away from mine ordinances, and have not kept them. Return unto me, and I will return unto you, saith the Lord of hosts. But ye said, Wherein shall we return? Will a man rob God? Yet ye have robbed me. But ye say, Wherein have we robbed thee? In tithes and offerings.
7. **Malachi 3:9** — Ye are cursed with a curse: for ye have robbed me, even this whole nation.
8. **Malachi 3:10** — Bring ye all the tithes into the storehouse, that there may be meat in mine house, and prove me now herewith, saith the

Lord of hosts, if I will not open you the windows of heaven, and pour you out a blessing, that there shall not be room enough to receive it.
9. **Genesis 7:11** — In the six hundredth year of Noah's life, in the second month, the seventeenth day of the month, the same day were all the fountains of the great deep broken up, and the windows of heaven were opened.
10. **Genesis 7:19** — And the waters prevailed exceedingly upon the earth; and all the high hills, that were under the whole heaven, were covered.
11. **Exodus 16:4** — ...Behold, I will rain bread from heaven for you....
12. **Psalm 78:23-25** — ...[God] opened the doors of heaven, and had rained down manna upon them to eat...and man did eat angels' food....
13. **Malachi 3:11** — And I will rebuke the devourer for your sakes, and he shall not destroy the fruits of your ground; neither shall your vine cast her fruit before the time in the field, saith the Lord of hosts.

GREEK WORDS
1. "where" — ὅπου (*hopou*): exactly where; in the place
2. "treasure" — θησαυρός (*thsauros*): a treasure; money, riches, or investments
3. "there" — ἐκεῖ (*ekei*): there; exactly there

SYNOPSIS
In the Old Testament, we see example after example of people building altars and then offering their sacrifices to God at critical moments in their lives. These gifts were not afterthoughts — they were planned, prepared, and well thought out. And as these sacrificial gifts were given, God was faithful to generously respond.

For example, after the flood, Noah built an altar and made a sacrifice to God. When Abraham found giants in the Promised Land, he built an altar and made a sacrifice to God. When there was a plague, David built an altar and made a sacrifice to God. When Solomon became king, he also built an altar and made a sacrifice to God.

Their generous sacrifices moved God to generously respond to their needs. And the greater their sacrifice, the greater the response was from God. This shows us, again, that what we sow, we will also reap — as well as the truth from Matthew 6:21 that where we put our money, our heart will also be.

The emphasis of this lesson:

When we give with the right heart attitude, the window of Heaven opens. And when the window of Heaven is open, the goodness of God pours into our life. As we are faithful to give God what belongs to Him, He will be faithful to bless us and meet our needs abundantly.

In Matthew 6:21, Jesus said, "For where your treasure is, there will your heart be also." The word "where" in Greek means *exactly there*, and the word "treasure" is the Greek word *thsauros*, which describes *treasure*, *money*, *riches*, *investments*, and *resources*. Jesus was saying that *exactly where* you put your *treasure* — your *money* and *resources* — is where your heart will be.

When you love someone, you invest in him or her. When you love the Kingdom of God, you invest in the Kingdom of God, and that is what Jesus is teaching in this verse. Money reveals our heart, so if you want to know where your heart is, just follow your money.

Giving With a Right Heart

One of the most important texts on giving is found in Malachi 1. In verses 7 and 8, God is listening to His people. God hears what we say to one another; He even hears what we privately think. We see evidence of that in these verses:

> **Ye offer polluted bread upon mine altar; and ye say, Wherein have we polluted thee? In that ye say, The table of the Lord is contemptible. And if ye offer the blind for sacrifice, is it not evil? and if ye offer the lame and sick, is it not evil? offer it now unto thy governor; will he be pleased with thee, or accept thy person? saith the Lord of hosts.**
> **— Malachi 1:7,8**

God's people were saying, "Ugh, we're so tired of giving, and we're so tired of hearing about giving. The table of the Lord is such a drudgery — we're so tired of this." They even called the table of the Lord *contemptible*.

In essence, God told them, "Your offerings are a stench to Me because of the attitude in which you offer them. In fact, by offering your sacrifice with such resentment, you've contaminated My altar. You are giving defective rejects — blind, lame, and sick animals — when you could be bringing Me the best. This is detestable to Me! Why, you wouldn't even do this to your governor! You're doing to Me what you wouldn't even do to him!"

The Israelites were offering God the leftovers they didn't want. They weren't real sacrifices because these sacrifices cost them nothing to give, and God knew that. God didn't need their animals, but He did want their hearts.

The gifts the Israelites brought revealed that their hearts were not right when it came to the subject of giving. In Malachi 1:10, God rebuked them, saying:

> **Who is there even among you that would shut the doors for nought? Neither do ye kindle fire on mine altar for nought. I have no pleasure in you, saith the Lord of hosts, neither will I accept an offering at your hand.**

God was essentially saying, "Shut the doors to My house! If you're going to treat Me so disrespectfully, then stay out of My presence. Don't bring inferior offerings that are an insult to Me and that clearly show the distance in your heart toward Me."

God didn't need the Israelites' offerings. He doesn't need our offerings either. God has always wanted His peoples' *hearts*. And just like Matthew 6:21 says, "…Where your treasure is, there will your heart be also." The inferior offerings the Israelites were bringing revealed that they had defective hearts.

Finally, God said:

> **But ye have profaned it, in that ye say, The table of the Lord is polluted; and the fruit thereof, even his meat, is contemptible.**
> — **Malachi 1:12**

The Israelites had grown tired of bringing offerings to God, and as a result, this verse says they polluted the table of the Lord, bringing defective and inferior sacrifices with a wrong heart.

Verse 13 goes on to say:

> **Ye said also, Behold, what a weariness is it! and ye have snuffed at it, saith the Lord of hosts; and ye brought that which was**

torn, and the lame, and the sick; thus ye brought an offering: should I accept this of your hand? saith the Lord.

These are very strong words, and they show how serious God is about the attitude of His people's hearts when they give their tithes and offerings to Him.

Although His language is strong, God knew that some people listening would want to make things right. In Malachi 3:7 and 8, He tells the Israelites how to do just that:

> **Even from the days of your fathers ye are gone away from mine ordinances, and have not kept them. Return unto me, and I will return unto you, saith the Lord of hosts. But ye said, Wherein shall we return? Will a man rob God? Yet ye have robbed me. But ye say, Wherein have we robbed thee? In tithes and offerings.**

First, God says, "…Return unto me, and I will return unto you…" (Malachi 3:7). Here we find a principle of Scripture — when we move toward God, He moves toward us. Although God rebuked Israel for its wrong heart and defective sacrifices, He urged the people to return to Him.

God went on to say, "…But ye said, Wherein shall we return? …In tithes and offerings" (Malachi 3:7,8). The Israelites had been robbing God by withholding proper sacrifices from Him. By refusing to obey God, they had also removed themselves from the realm of His blessing. God was trying to tell them, "Return to Me the right way, with right hearts and the offerings I deserve, and I will return to you."

A Self-Imposed Curse

As Rick shared previously, he and Denise did not regularly give when they were first married. Rick did not have faith to believe for finances, so he was not obedient to tithe or give. He hated when their pastor would teach on these verses from Malachi because he knew he was robbing God. Denise would even ask, "Rick, are we tithing? Are we giving?" And Rick would try to deflect her question because he knew they weren't.

Because Rick did not have a revelation about giving, he and Denise were cursed in their lives. They faced many challenges. God didn't curse them — it was a self-imposed curse. By not giving, Rick had removed them from the realm where God could bless them. We see an example of this in Malachi 3:9:

Ye are cursed with a curse: for ye have robbed me, even this whole nation.

Because of the Israelites' wrong hearts and incorrect actions, the entire nation had come under a self-imposed curse. When we rob God of what belongs to Him, it removes us from the realm of His blessings and thrusts us into a realm where we begin to reap negative things. This verse does not say God brought a curse — it is cautioning us to recognize that if we refuse to obey God's biblical principles, we remove ourselves from the blessing that would otherwise be ours.

It is the principle of sowing and reaping. What a man sows, he will also reap. If a farmer never puts seed into the soil, eventually nothing will be produced by the soil, and he will be cursed due to his lack of investment. And in the same way, when you do not release your finances into the Kingdom of God, a day is going to come when you run out of finances and are cursed. It won't be because God cursed you; it will be because you did not participate in the law of sowing and reaping.

That is exactly what happened to Rick and Denise in the early days of their ministry. They were cursed and lived their lives at a very low level. Not only were they cursed, they also had friends who were cursed, and none of them had a revelation about giving.

Rick remembers one week he ran out of gas five times because he only had enough money to put one dollar of gas at a time into the tank of his car. He was humiliated having to call someone five times from a pay phone to ask, "Can you please have mercy on me and bring some gas for my car? This happened *five times* in one week!

At the time, Rick and Denise were living low-level lives because they were not giving. It was a self-imposed curse, just like Malachi 3:9 says. **But God does not want any of His people to be cursed.**

If you're having financial difficulty or other problems in your life, the issue may be that you've removed yourself from the sphere of God's blessing and, as a result, the enemy has accessed your life. Of course, this does *not* mean that every financial difficulty, struggle, or setback means a person has done wrong in regard to giving. But if you realize you are struggling financially and you're living with a deficit, you may need to ask, "God, am I giving as I'm supposed to be giving?"

If you are sowing and still have a problem with your finances, then you probably need to deal with the devil. The devil will oppose *any* promised blessing in our lives, but you have the authority to tell the devil to move off your finances.

Look at what God says in Malachi 3:10:

> **Bring ye all the tithes into the storehouse, that there may be meat in mine house, and prove me now herewith, saith the Lord of hosts, if I will not open you the windows of heaven, and pour you out a blessing, that there shall not be room enough to receive it.**

God is saying, "Give Me a chance to show you what I'll do." He wants to open the windows of Heaven and "pour you out a blessing, that there shall not be room enough to receive it" (Malachi 3:10).

That's what God wants to do. He is not trying to get something *from* you; He's trying to get something *to* you. And what God wants to give you is *abundant*. There will not even be room enough to receive it.

The Window of Heaven

What is "the window of Heaven"? The window of Heaven appears three times in the Old Testament: Genesis 7:11, Psalm 78:23, and Malachi 3:10. In order to better understand what the window of Heaven is, we're going to take a closer look at what happens when it opens and what happens when it does not.

The first mention of the window of Heaven is in Genesis 7:11:

> **In the six hundredth year of Noah's life, in the second month, the seventeenth day of the month, the same day were all the fountains of the great deep broken up, and the windows of heaven were opened.**

What happened when the window of Heaven opened? When that window opened, rain started pouring through. It kept raining for 40 days and nights, and later we find that "…the waters prevailed exceedingly upon the earth; and all the high hills, that were under the whole heaven, were covered" (Genesis 7:19).

The first time the window of Heaven opened in Scripture, so much rain came pouring through that the earth was flooded! It was miraculous the level of abundance that came pouring through the opened window of Heaven. We will continue to see that anytime the window of Heaven opens, miraculous things happen and abundance comes pouring through.

The second time the window of Heaven opened in Scripture was while the children of Israel were wandering in the wilderness. They had walked through the wilderness for two months, long enough for their food supply to run low, and they began complaining about their situation.

In Exodus 16:4, God told the Israelites, "…Behold, I will rain bread from heaven for you…." And God not only provided manna — He provided it abundantly!

> **…[God] opened the doors of heaven, and had rained down manna upon them to eat…and man did eat angels' food….**
> **— Psalm 78:23-25**

The Psalmist tells us first that the *windows* — or doors — *of heaven* opened (Psalm 78:23), and when the windows of heaven opened, manna *rained* down on them (v. 24). The phrase "the doors of Heaven" refers to the "windows of Heaven" — a heavenly portal — that opens at God's command. And when that window opened, so much manna *rained down* that the Israelites did not have enough room to receive it all.

Rabbinical literature says manna fell in such abundance every day that it spread over more than 2,000 square cubits with a depth of 50 to 60 cubits. *If* this was the case, a single day's supply of manna would have been enough to feed the children of Israel for 2,000 years. God gave them far more than they needed.

It is impossible to know exactly how much manna came pouring through the open window of Heaven during those 40 years, but rabbis have made this rough estimate. If the Israelites numbered approximately 3 million people, as many Bible scholars believe, it is estimated that they would have needed 4,500 tons of manna every day. If they gathered 4,500 tons of manna every day for 40 years, that means an estimated 65,700,000 tons of manna supernaturally appeared on the ground over that period of time. That is incredible!

Imagine if you woke up tomorrow morning to find 4,500 tons of beautiful, freshly baked manna lying on the ground all over your city — free to anyone who wanted to go out and pick it up and take it home. It would be a worldwide sensation. Scientists would fly in from around the world to study it, journalists would write about it, and every major news program would cover the story.

This miracle happened for the children of Israel every day for 40 years. An entire generation of Israelite children grew up in the wilderness thinking it was normal to wake up and miraculously find 4,500 tons of manna lying on the ground. They didn't even know life without this supernatural provision. That's what happened when the window of Heaven opened over the children of Israel.

So far, we have seen the window of Heaven open and abundantly rain in Genesis 7 and miraculously pour out manna in Exodus 16:4 and Psalm 78:23-25. Now let's return to Malachi 3:10:

> **Bring ye all the tithes into the storehouse, that there may be meat in mine house, and prove me now herewith, saith the Lord of hosts, if I will not open you the windows of heaven, and pour you out a blessing, that there shall not be room enough to receive it.**

In this verse, God promises to open the windows of Heaven to those who bring "all the tithes" into His storehouse. He is promising to open the window and *abundantly* pour out blessings on those who willingly give to Him. And God promises to do it so much that they will not even have enough room to receive it all!

Rather than saying, "God, I'm giving so You'll meet this little need in my life. Could You give me just enough?" we need to upgrade our faith. God wants to fill your life until it is overflowing! He wants to open the window of Heaven over your life to such a degree that you will not have room to receive everything that He wants to give. We need to renew our minds to that truth — God wants to abundantly bless you with *more than enough*. And He doesn't stop there.

> **And I will rebuke the devourer for your sakes, and he shall not destroy the fruits of your ground; neither shall your vine cast her fruit before the time in the field, saith the Lord of hosts.**
> — Malachi 3:11

When we open our hands to give, God opens His mouth. He rebukes the devil on our behalf, saying, "Move off that person. That person is a generous giver. Move off of him (or her) right now." And when God speaks to the devil, the devil moves — that is the truth!

Looking back at Malachi 1 and 3, we see that God is listening to us, and He knows our heart and the attitude we have when we give. He also goes on to tell us how to return to Him and make things right regarding our giving. He tells us to bring a generous offering into the house of God and that, as a result, He will open the window of Heaven over our life and pour out a blessing so huge we won't even know how to contain it all. And He will open His mouth to tell the devil to move off our life. All of these promises belong to those who generously give.

If you have made a mistake in this area of your life, repent and ask God what you need to give and where it should go. God wants to bless you abundantly! Open up your heart and your wallet to Him and see what He will do.

STUDY QUESTIONS

> **Study to shew thyself approved unto God, a workman that needeth not to be ashamed, rightly dividing the word of truth.**
> — 2 Timothy 2:15

1. What is the difference between a right heart and a wrong heart when you give?
2. What were the Israelites doing wrong in Malachi 1? How did God say they could fix their situation in Malachi 3?
3. Rick shared about how he and Denise were living cursed lives when they were first married. Why was that? What did they do to change their situation?
4. When we tithe and bring God what belongs to Him, what does He say He will do for us in Malachi 3:11?

PRACTICAL APPLICATION

> But be ye doers of the word, and not hearers only, deceiving your own selves.
> —James 1:22

1. Have you been living a low-level life because you're not giving? If so, repent and ask God what you can give and where it should go. Remember, God doesn't want something *from* you; He's trying to get something *to* you. And when you give, you allow Him to do just that.
2. Sometimes in life we grow comfortable with having just enough, but that's not God's desire for you. He wants you to have *more* than enough. Ask the Holy Spirit if there is any place in your life where you could use a faith upgrade.
3. Has there been a moment when God met your need abundantly? Write it down and thank Him for His faithful provision in your life.

LESSON 4

TOPIC
What Jesus Said About Giving

SCRIPTURES

1. **Matthew 6:21** — For where your treasure is, there will your heart be also.
2. **Luke 21:1** — And he looked up, and saw the rich men casting their gifts into the treasury.
3. **Luke 21:2** — And he saw also a certain poor widow casting in thither two mites.
4. **Luke 21:3** — And he said, Of a truth I say unto you, that this poor widow hath cast in more than they all.
5. **Luke 21:4** — For all these have of their abundance cast in unto the offerings of God: but she of her penury hath cast in all the living that she had.

GREEK WORDS

1. "where" — ὅπου (*hopou*): exactly where; in the place
2. "treasure" — θησαυρός (*thsauros*): a treasure; money, riches, or investments
3. "there" — ἐκεῖ (*ekei*): there; exactly there
4. "saw" — ὁράω (*horao*): a scrutinizing look; to look with the intent to examine
5. "rich men" — πλουσίους (*plousious*): plural, many very rich people
6. "casting" — βάλλω (*ballo*): to throw, to toss, or to throw an object
7. "gifts" — δῶρα (*dora*): plural, gifts or contributions
8. "treasury" — γαζοφυλάκιον (*radzophulakion*): treasury; not offerings, but into the repository for contributions
9. "also" — δέ (*de*): used as a marker of comparison and exclamation
10. "poor" — πενιχρός (*penichros*): depicts a person living in abject poverty; a needy person; one so poor that he often lives by begging
11. "in" — ἐκεῖ (*ekei*): there; exactly there; very aware of where she was placing her offering
12. "mites" — λεπτόν (*lepton*): a small coin made of brass and worth very little
13. "of a truth" — ἀληθῶς (*alelthos*): truly; certainly; surely; in reality
14. "that" — ὅτι (*hoti*): points to an express statement
15. "poor" — πτωχός (*ptochos*): deeply destitute; completely lacking resources; embarrassingly poor; a pauper; one who crouches in embarrassment
16. "more than" [they all] — πλεῖον (*pleion*): an adjective meaning greater in quantity; numerically more; something of a much greater value; comparatively more
17. "of their abundance" — ἐκ τοῦ περισσεύοντος (*ek tou peisseuontos*): out of their excess; out of their overflowing excess
18. "but" — δέ (*de*): used as a marker of comparison and exclamation
19. "of her penury" — ἐκ τοῦ ὑστερήματος (*ek tou husterematos*): out of her lack; out of her deficit; out of her insufficiency
20. "all" — πάντα (*panta*): all encompassing; literally everything
21. "living" — βίον (*bion*): from βίος (bios); life; everything she needs to live
22. "had" — ἔχω (*echo*): to have, hold, or to possess

SYNOPSIS

In Lesson 1 we learned that God is generous with those who are generous. In Lesson 2 we saw how God responds supernaturally to sacrificial giving, and in Lesson 3 we saw how to open the window of Heaven over our life.

Every time the window of Heaven opened in the Old Testament, something miraculous came pouring through it. That's why Malachi 3:10 says God *wants* to open the window of Heaven over our life and pour out a blessing so big we won't have room to receive it all.

We need to upgrade our faith and realize God wants to do much more than simply meet our needs. He wants to *flood* our lives with His goodness in response to our giving.

The emphasis of this lesson:

When we give, Jesus is watching. Whether we give a lot or a little, He is looking at our heart to see what we are bringing to Him and how we are doing it. Jesus is clear that what we bring matters just as much as the faith and reverence we give it with.

In Matthew 6:21, Jesus says, "For where your treasure is, there will your heart be also." This verse may seem simplistic at first, but it reveals an important truth about our lives. What we do with our money reveals where our heart is. Jesus was saying that where we put our treasure — *exactly there, in the very place* — is where our heart is.

It's not difficult to figure out where a person's heart is. You just need to follow his or her money and you'll find the truth of what that individual highly values in life.

Jesus Watches How and What We Give

In Luke 21, Jesus was standing in the Temple, watching *how* and *what* people gave. He was standing so close to the treasury that He could even see the amount they were putting in. Imagine if the offering plate was being passed down the aisles at your church and your pastor followed the plate as it passed from hand to hand. That would be strange!

Although it is hard to imagine what Jesus was doing, He was looking to see the reverence with which people were giving — were they giving with faith or just casually giving? What were they giving? Were they really obeying God with their money? Jesus was watching all of it. And the Bible tells us in Luke 21:1:

> **And he looked up, and saw the rich men casting their gifts into the treasury.**

The word "saw" is a form of the Greek word *horao*, which describes *a scrutinizing look* or *to look with the intent to examine*. Jesus was really examining what people were giving, and according to Hebrews 13:8, He is still examining our giving today. When we give, Jesus is looking to see if we are giving with a right attitude.

This verse tells us Jesus specifically saw the rich men. He drew near to examine what they were giving. The word "rich" is a form of the Greek word *plousious*, and it describes people who are fabulously wealthy.

Jesus watched the rich men and saw how they were casting their gifts into the treasury. The word "casting" that is used here means *to toss* or *to throw an object*. It tells us something about their attitude towards giving. These men were not reverently bringing their money to give; they were just throwing it in casually as they walked by. It required no faith. They were simply casting their excess into the treasury.

The word "treasury" is also important. It is the Greek word *radzophulakion*, which depicts the place where contributions were kept. These were not offerings — it wasn't something sacrificial or reverential for the rich men. They were just tossing excess funds into the place the contributions were kept.

We can be pretty sure that these men were giving something like silver coins, which was pretty valuable currency, but they were *plousious* — very wealthy — men. They were not giving what they should have been giving, and they were not giving with the right attitude. And Jesus watched them with a scrutinizing gaze to see how they were giving and exactly what they were giving.

The Bible goes on to say:

> **And he saw also a certain poor widow casting in thither two mites.**
>
> — Luke 21:2

The word "saw" is the same word used in verse 1, a form of the Greek word *horao*, describing *a scrutinizing look* or *to look with the intention to examine*. Jesus drew near when He saw this poor widow. He examined her closely as she gave to see what kind of attitude she had and what she brought to give.

This verse says Jesus saw "also." In Greek, the word "also" is a translation of the word *de*, which is used here as an exclamation marker. After seeing one rich man after another toss their money in with no reverence — no faith — the sight of this poor widow really got Jesus' attention.

The word "poor" is a translation of the Greek word *penichros*. There are several words for "poor" in the Greek language, but this particular word depicts *a person living in abject poverty* or *one so poor that he or she often lives by begging*. This widow was not just a poor person. She was living in abject poverty and possibly made her living by begging. And we are told Jesus saw her "also" — remarkably, emphatically, like an exclamation mark — "casting in thither two mites" (Luke 21:2).

The word "in" is a translation of the Greek word *ekei*, meaning *exactly there*. She was very aware of where she was placing her offering, unlike the rich men who casually walked by and tossed in their money. It was a great, great sacrifice for this woman to place her gift in the treasury, and the Bible says she placed there "two mites" (Luke 21:2).

You may be wondering, what is a mite? It was a small coin made of brass, and it was worth very, very little. It was the smallest and the least valuable coin in the currency of that day. To the natural eye, it probably looked like this woman gave very little because it wasn't worth much. But look at what Jesus had to say about it in verse 3:

> **And he said, Of a truth I say unto you, that this poor widow hath cast in more than they all.**
> — **Luke 21:3**

Jesus was so impressed with what this woman gave and the way that she gave — the enormity of her faith and the reverence with which she placed it into the treasury that He stopped everything and said, "Stop, stop, stop! I need to make a statement." He'd been watching the way she gave and the two brass coins in her hand, and Jesus said, "Look at this woman. She is giving more than you all."

That statement probably shocked those listening. One rich man after another was tossing in silver coins while this poor woman gave only two mites. But Jesus stopped and said, "…Of a truth…" (Luke 21:3). In Greek this is the word *alelthos* which means *truly, certainly, surely,* or *in reality.* Jesus was saying, "*In reality,* this is what is true."

Jesus went on to say, "…I say unto you, *that*…" (Luke 21:3). The word "that" is the Greek word *hoti,* which points to an express statement. Jesus was getting ready to point out something very important.

Jesus continued, "…This poor widow…" (Luke 21:3), and here He used another word for "poor." This is the Greek word *ptochos,* meaning *one that is deeply destitute, completely lacking resources, or embarrassingly poor.* It depicts someone who crouches in embarrassment because of his or her poverty.

This was a woman with pride and dignity. She was embarrassingly poor, but she came up to the place where the contributions were made and, in spite of her destitute condition, she cast in her two mites with great faith and reverence. And watching this, Jesus said, "…Of a truth I say unto you, that this poor widow hath cast in more than they all" (Luke 21:3).

The phrase "more than they all" in Greek is an adjective meaning *greater in quantity, numerically more,* or *something of a much greater value.* Even though the poor widow only placed two mites into the treasury, Jesus was literally saying that her gift was worth more than all the contributions of the rich men combined.

We know that naturally speaking, two mites were worth a lot less than many silver coins, so what did Jesus mean? He tells us in verse 4:

> **For all these have of their abundance cast in unto the offerings of God: but she of her penury hath cast in all the living that she had.**
> **— Luke 21:4**

When Jesus said, "…These have of their abundance…," the Greek literally means *out of their excess.* It could be translated, *out of their overflowing excess* these rich men have just randomly, casually, "cast in unto the offerings of God" (Luke 21:4).

Then Jesus said, "…But she of her penury…" (Luke 21:4). "But" is, again, the Greek word *de,* acting as an exclamation marker. It's like Jesus was saying, "Wow! Look at this! This is amazing." The word "penury" is a translation of a form of the Greek word *hustereos,* and a better translation here would be *out of her lack*, *out of her deficit*, or *out of her insufficiency*. This was a woman who had great lack in her life, and Jesus said she cast in *all*.

The word "all" is a translation of the Greek word *panta*, a compound of the words *pan* and *ta*. The word *pan* means *all-encompassing*, and the word *ta* describes every little detail, literally meaning *everything*. Compounded together, *panta* means *all-encompassing* or *all-inclusive*. When Jesus said this woman "cast in *all*," He was recognizing that she had given everything, she gave all her *living* (Luke 21:4).

The word "living" in this verse is the Greek word *bion*, which is a form of the Greek word *bios*. The word *bios* is the word for *life*, and when it becomes the word *bion*, it means *everything she had that was required for living*. This poor woman gave reverentially and sacrificially; in fact, Jesus said she gave "all the living that she had" (Luke 21:4).

The word "had" is a form of the Greek word *echo*, which means *to have*, *to hold*, or *to possess*. So we see, again, that this woman put everything she had into that offering. And Jesus said because of her faith and because of the level of sacrifice she was making, what she gave was worth more than all the gifts of the rich men combined.

Hers was a greater sacrifice. The rich men didn't even scratch the surface of their fortunes with the amount they gave, so they were able to give their offerings without much personal sacrifice or faith, but this poor woman gave everything. She had barely enough to survive, and she chose to give it all in faith.

Another Great Sacrifice

The woman from this verse reminded Rick of his Grandmother Bagley. She was an uneducated woman who faced a lot of hardship in her life, but Rick loved her dearly.

He remembers eating at her house one day and asking her for seconds. She had made fried pork, and it was so delicious that he couldn't help but ask for more. She said to him, "Ricky, your Grandmother Bagley doesn't have a lot of money, and today you're going to have to be happy with what you had because I don't have enough to give you seconds." Hearing that, Rick remembers thinking, *Wow, my grandmother really doesn't have much.*

Later the same day, Rick saw his grandmother do something he'll never forget. She took an envelope and wrote the name *Oral Roberts* on the front. She was so uneducated that she couldn't write very well, but she scribbled the name *Oral Roberts* on the envelope as well as she could. Then Rick saw her take a single dollar bill and place it into the envelope. She licked and sealed the envelope then held it next to her heart and prayed. Lastly, she went outside and put that envelope in the mailbox for the mailman to pick up.

To Rick's grandmother, one dollar was a great, great sacrifice, and seeing the way his Grandmother Bagley gave that one dollar impressed Rick deeply. It is a memory that has stayed with him all his life. It reminded him — and it is a reminder to us all — that some people who give smaller gifts actually give with greater sacrifice and faith than those with very large gifts. This is not to say that rich people cannot also be generous givers — there are definitely rich people who are very generous, sacrificial givers — but sometimes the gifts of people who don't have a lot seem small in comparison. It is important for us to remember that for people who don't have much, it takes an even greater level of faith to give.

That is what the poor widow was like. Jesus watched her come and give her two mites, and He was so impressed with how and what she gave that He said, "Stop, stop, stop. You all need to see what just happened." He pointed out her example of how to truly give with great sacrifice and great faith.

Remember, Jesus is still watching how and what we give today. He is looking for what kind of reverence and faith we have when we give. He is also looking at the amount that we give because the amount is also important. But this, again, is because God is after our heart (*see* Matthew 6:21).

The Result of Giving

In Lesson 1, we covered how it's possible to give without loving. We see an example of this, again, with the rich men in Luke 21. They were simply giving to fulfill a duty or obligation; they were not using their faith or taking time to bring God the best of what they had. But the poor widow did. She gave everything she had to the Lord and demonstrated that her heart was in the Kingdom of God.

We don't know from Scripture what happened to this poor woman, but we do know that God is generous with the generous. We know that He especially blesses sacrificial giving, and we have also seen that God responds to what we bring into His house — He opens the window of Heaven over our lives.

Although the Bible doesn't tell us what happened, we can be sure that God was generous with this woman. It may be that she was giving in faith, believing for the window of Heaven to open over her life. And that is what happens when we give correctly, with a right attitude, and when we give the amount God has asked us to give.

STUDY QUESTIONS

> Study to shew thyself approved unto God, a workman that needeth not to be ashamed, rightly dividing the word of truth.
> — 2 Timothy 2:15

1. What was wrong with the offering of the rich men in Luke 21? What issue did Jesus have with how and what they gave?
2. What impressed Jesus about the poor widow? What did Jesus tell the other people in the Temple to take note of?
3. What do you think happened to the poor widow from Luke 21? Considering what we've covered in previous lessons about what the Bible has to say about giving, what might her life have looked like after such a faith-filled offering?

PRACTICAL APPLICATION

> But be ye doers of the word, and not hearers only, deceiving your own selves.
> — James 1:22

1. What if Jesus was literally standing in front of you as you gave? How would you feel? What do you think He would say?
2. Are there people in your life that you look up to because of how they give? Who could you imitate to grow your reverence and faith in how you give?
3. What impact do you think it would have in your own life to give an offering like the poor widow from Luke 21 gave?

LESSON 5

TOPIC
What the Apostle Paul Said About Giving

SCRIPTURES
1. **Matthew 6:21** — For where your treasure is, there will your heart be also.
2. **2 Corinthians 8:1** — Moreover, brethren, we do you to wit of the grace of God bestowed on the churches of Macedonia.
3. **2 Corinthians 8:2** — How that in a great trial of affliction the abundance of their joy and their deep poverty abounded unto the riches of their liberality.
4. **2 Corinthians 8:3** — For to their power, I bear record, yea, and beyond their power they were willing of themselves.
5. **2 Corinthians 8:4** — Praying us with much intreaty that we would receive the gift, and take upon us the fellowship of the ministering to the saints.
6. **2 Corinthians 8:5** — And this they did, not as we hoped, but first gave their own selves to the Lord, and unto us by the will of God.
7. **Philippians 4:19** — But my God shall supply all your need according to his riches in glory by Christ Jesus.

GREEK WORDS
1. "where" — ὅπου (*hopou*): exactly where; in the place
2. "treasure" — θησαυρός (*thsauros*): a treasure; money, riches, or investments
3. "there" — ἐκεῖ (*ekei*): there; exactly there
4. "deep poverty" — κατὰ βάθους πτωχεία (*kata bathous ptocheia*): being crushed by an embarrassing, deep level of poverty and completely lacking in resources
5. "abounded" — περισσεύω (*perisseuo*): to abound; to overflow like a river that crests its banks and spills over

6. "unto the riches of their liberality" — εἰς τὸ πλοῦτος ἀπλότητος αὐτῶν (*eis to ploutos apolotetos auton*): into the fabulous riches of their bountiful generosity
7. "for to their power" — ὅτι κατὰ δύναμιν (*hoti kata dunamin*): that according to their ability
8. "beyond their power" — παρὰ δύναμιν (*para dunamin*): way beyond their ability; way outside of their power
9. "willing" — αὐθαίρετος (*authairetos*): self-willing; by their own choice; voluntarily
10. "praying" — δέομαι (*deomai*): beg; implore; plead
11. "much entreaty" — πολλῆς παρακλήσεω (*polles parakleseo*): a lot of pleading; a lot of begging

SYNOPSIS

We have seen many examples of giving in Scripture. We learned that God is generous with the generous, we found that God marvelously responds to sacrificial giving, we saw how to open the window of Heaven over our lives and what happens when that window is opened, and, finally in Lesson 4, we discovered what Jesus had to say about generosity and giving.

What we bring to give to God and *how* we give matters. Our attitude and faith about giving has the ability to grab the attention of Jesus and leave Him in awe. This is not something we should take lightly. Jesus is always watching to see what we give, but we have to decide to take it seriously.

Yesterday we saw what Jesus had to say about generosity and giving, and in today's lesson, we'll see what the apostle Paul had to say about it.

The emphasis of this lesson:

It is plainly written in Scripture that what we sow we will also reap. These powerful words of the apostle Paul remind us that God generously blesses those who willingly give what they have. The churches of Macedonia did this and through their financial gift, they gained access to the supernatural supply of God.

The Law of Sowing and Reaping

One of the most important verses written by the apostle Paul about giving is Galatians 6:7: "Be not deceived; God is not mocked: for whatsoever a man soweth, that shall he also reap."

Paul made several impactful statements here. First, he said, "Be not deceived…," meaning don't let anyone lead you astray on this subject. Then he said, "…God is not mocked…" to clarify even further that he was about to share a spiritual truth that can never violated or altered. Finally, Paul said, "…For whatsoever a man soweth, that shall he also reap" — this is the law of sowing and reaping (Galatians 6:7).

Paul wanted to make certain the believers he was writing to understood that whatever they gave would be returned to them, whether they were giving much or giving little. And this spiritual law applies to more than just giving money. If you sow love, you'll reap love. If you sow forgiveness, you'll have a harvest of forgiveness. If you sow mercy, you'll reap mercy, and so on. It doesn't matter what it is — whatever you sow, you're going to reap.

The Greek translation of this verse is very important because the tense used here actually means that whatever a man sows and sows and sows. It doesn't describe a one-time sowing but a habitual, continuous sowing, again and again.

The word "that" is very emphatic in Greek. It translates to mean *that* very thing he sowed, *that* is the very thing he is going to reap. If you sow patience, you're going to also reap *patience*, and if you sow finances, you're going to reap *finances*.

In this verse, the word "reap" also uses the same Greek tense as the word "sow." So, essentially, you could say, whatever you sow and sow and sow, that is what you're going to reap and reap and reap. This tells us that the *measure* to which we sow and the *regularity* with which we sow determines the measure that we reap and the regularity with which we reap.

Your sowing determines your reaping. If you sow consistently all the time, you're going to reap consistently all the time.

Paul Rebukes the Church of Corinth

The city of Corinth was a very prosperous city, and many believers there had ample amounts of money. Interestingly, it appears that believers in Corinth didn't suffer financially like believers did in other places.

At one point, the believers in Corinth announced that they were going to give a huge, sacrificial gift toward the apostle Paul's ministry. Paul shared news of this to other churches he went to, and after some time, word of the Corinthians' generosity began to spread all throughout the First Century church. But there was one problem — the Corinthians forgot that they made the promise and never gave.

Can you imagine that? Paul had been telling all these other churches about what the Corinthians were going to do, and then they never did it. So in Second Corinthians 8:1-5, Paul wrote to them and reminded them to follow through on their promise.

> **Moreover, brethren, we do you to wit of the grace of God bestowed on the churches of Macedonia.**
> **— 2 Corinthians 8:1**

Paul began by telling the Corinthians about the sacrificial giving of believers elsewhere. He essentially said, "Let me give you the example of the Macedonians who didn't just intend to give, they *did* give." Notice how Paul describes the churches of Macedonia in verse 2:

> **How that in a great trial of affliction the abundance of their joy and their deep poverty abounded unto the riches of their liberality.**
> **— 2 Corinthians 8:2**

Paul writes that the "deep poverty" of the churches in Macedonia "abounded" (2 Corinthians 8:2). The words "deep poverty" in Greek literally means *being crushed by an embarrassing, deep level of poverty and completely lacking in resources*. That was the reality of the churches of Macedonia, which were also known as the churches of Philippi.

These believers were under great, great stress and intense persecution. Many of them had lost their jobs and with that, they had lost their income; many had also lost their homes. They were really suffering because of their faith in Jesus.

Yet even though the Macedonians had lost so much, verse 2 tells us that their heart was in the Kingdom of God. Just like Matthew 6:21 says, they invested their money in the spreading of the Gospel because that was where their heart was.

Paul says they "...abounded unto the riches of their liberality" (2 Corinthians 8:2). The word "abounded" in Greek means *to overflow like a river that is cresting its banks and spilling over*. In other words, this word describes fabulous riches or bountiful generosity.

These believers who were suffering persecution, who had lost their jobs, and who had even lost their homes on account of their faith in Christ pooled together what resources they did have to give a significant offering to the apostle Paul. Because their hearts were in the Kingdom of God, they were unbelievably generous as Paul said, "...unto the riches of their liberality" (2 Corinthians 8:2).

Paul comments on their generosity in verse 3:

> **For to their power, I bear record, yea, and beyond their power they were willing of themselves.**
> **— 2 Corinthians 8:3**

The *King James Version* does not translate the meaning of this verse well — it really misses the point. For example, where the verse says, "For to their power...," the Greek actually says *for according to their ability* (2 Corinthians 8:3). The verse goes on to say, "...And beyond their power...," and the Greek says *way beyond their ability* or *way outside of their power*.

In this verse, Paul was saying that the Macedonians gave what they could according to their own ability, but their hearts were so in the Kingdom of God that they were willing to give even beyond that. It was supernatural what they gave — why? Because, they were *"willing* of themselves" (2 Corinthians 8:3). The word "willing" in Greek means they chose to do it *voluntarily* or *by their own choice*, not by coercion.

They wanted to see the advancement of the Gospel so they pooled all their resources to give the biggest offering they could possibly give. And Paul literally says they did it according to their ability and even beyond their ability because they wanted to do it.

Paul went on to say:

> **Praying us with much intreaty that we would receive the gift, and take upon us the fellowship of the ministering to the saints.**
> — **2 Corinthians 8:4**

There's so much inside this verse. The word "praying" is a form of the Greek word *deomai*, which means *to beg*, *to implore*, or *to plead*. Paul knew the destitute financial condition that the churches of Macedonia were in, and this verse tells us that when Paul heard what they were going to give him for the ministry, he probably said, "Guys, you keep it. You need this money." But the Macedonian believers *begged* him, *implored* him, and *pleaded* with him to receive their gift.

They might have said, "What do you mean you're not going to accept our gift? You teach us that if we sow, we will reap. How can you not accept this gift?" These believers begged, implored, and pleaded with Paul to receive the gift. In fact, Paul said they did it with "much intreaty," which means with *a lot of pleading* or *a lot of begging*.

They were sowing out of their deficit, out of their need; they were doing what they needed to do to open the window of Heaven over their lives to change their financial situation. And in verse 5, Paul continued:

> **And this they did, not as we hoped, but first gave their own selves to the Lord, and unto us by the will of God.**
> — **2 Corinthians 8:5**

Notice it says they "first gave their own selves to the Lord" (2 Corinthians 8:5). The Macedonian believers had given themselves first to the Lord, meaning they had made Jesus Lord of their lives. And when Jesus is Lord of your life, it means you've given everything you have to Him and now you're at His disposal to do whatever He asks.

When you call Jesus Lord of your life, you're saying He is Lord of you. He is Lord of your marriage, He is Lord of your relationships, He is Lord of your job, He is Lord of your salary, and He is Lord of your giving.

Paul was stunned that the Macedonians gave such an enormous gift, but in this verse, he recognized that they had given themselves to the Lord and the Lord was instructing them to do it. It was to these same generous believers that Paul later wrote:

> **But my God shall supply all your need according to his riches in glory by Christ Jesus.**
> — Philippians 4:19

This verse specifically holds a promise for *givers*. Paul was writing to the churches of Macedonia, to the Philippians, who had generously and sacrificially given. He wrote this in response to their generous gift. Paul wanted them to know that because they made the decision to be generous, God would generously meet their needs in response.

Taking into account the original Greek meaning, here is the *Renner Interpretive Version* (*RIV*) of Philippians 4:19:

> **But my God will supply your needs so completely that He will eliminate all your deficiencies. He will meet all your physical and tangible needs until you are so full that you have no more capacity to hold anything else. He will supply all your needs until you are totally filled, packed full and overflowing to the point of bursting at the seams and spilling over.**

This agrees with what we saw in Lesson 3 that when we bring generous gifts to God, it opens the windows of heaven and God pours out a blessing so big that we don't even have room enough to receive it.

No wonder Malachi 3:10 records God in essence saying, "Prove Me, give Me an opportunity to show you what I'll do if you'll just bring your generous gifts to Me. I will open the windows of heaven and pour out so much you'll be bursting at the seams."

Invest in Eternal Things

It is amazing that the churches of Macedonia pooled their resources and gave such a generous gift. And it's even more amazing that when the apostle Paul said, "Just keep it — you need it more than me," they responded, "No! You taught us to give, and we're going to give. *Please* receive it." They decided they were going to sow so that they could reap.

According to Matthew 6:21, what we do with our money reveals the condition of our heart. Jesus said that we will put our treasure where our heart is. The heart of the churches of Macedonia were in the Kingdom of God, and they proved this by giving a generous gift to Paul for his ministry.

The Corinthians made a big promise to give, but they never followed through. Paul then chides them in Second Corinthians 8 by giving them the example of the Macedonians', or the Philippians', generosity. The Macedonians were faithful even when they didn't have much because they knew giving would turn their situation around.

Martin Luther said these powerful words:

I have held many things in my hand, and have lost them all, but whatever I have placed in God's hands, that I still possess.

These words are so powerful. Material things are short-lived, and eventually they run out or we lose them. But the things we place into God's hand, for eternal purposes, never leave us. We have them forever.

What About You?

Have you been faithful in giving? Are you generously and sacrificially sowing into God's Kingdom without reservation? If you are not — *get started!*

Make a decision that you're going to begin today. If you are not a giver to your church, become a giver to your church. If you are not a partner, become a partner. As you dedicate yourself to be faithful in giving day by day, week by week, month by month, and year by year, you'll continue to grow in the grace of giving.

Remember, as you open your heart and your finances to God, He will be even more generous in meeting your needs because — ***God answers generosity with generosity.***

Your obedience to give will open the door for God to pour out His blessings on you, and when you begin to worship God with your finances, you acquire the right to claim the promise in Philippians 4:19 that God will abundantly "supply all your need according to his riches in glory by Christ Jesus."

STUDY QUESTIONS

> Study to shew thyself approved unto God, a workman that needeth not to be ashamed, rightly dividing the word of truth.
> — 2 Timothy 2:15

1. According to Galatians 6:7, how often do we need to sow in order to reap continually?
2. Why was it interesting that Paul used the word "praying" in Second Corinthians 8:4 to describe the Macedonian believers?
3. Who does Paul say was leading the Macedonian churches to give such a generous gift? (*See* 2 Corinthians 8:5.) Did Paul want to receive their gift?
4. What does Philippians 4:19 say the churches of Macedonia received in return for their generous gift? Notice this is the same promise God gives in Malachi 3:10.

PRACTICAL APPLICATION

> But be ye doers of the word, and not hearers only,
> deceiving your own selves.
> —James 1:22

1. Is there a financial gift that you committed to but forgot to actually give? If so, take the steps you need to in order to fulfill your promise.
2. What are two things we can learn from the example of the Macedonian believers' generosity? How does that challenge you in your own giving?
3. If you are not currently giving, what is one practical step you can take toward beginning to give today? Write it down and commit to do it this week.

Notes

Notes

Notes

CLAIM YOUR FREE RESOURCE!

As a way of introducing you further to the teaching ministry of Rick Renner, we would like to send you free of charge his teaching CD, "How To Receive a Miraculous Touch From God."

In His earthly ministry, Jesus commonly healed *all* who were sick of *all* their diseases. In this profound message, learn about the manifold dimensions of Christ's wisdom, goodness, power, and love toward all humanity who came to Him in faith with their needs.

☑ **YES, I want to receive Rick Renner's monthly teaching letter!**

Simply scan the QR code to claim this resource or go to:
renner.org/claim-your-free-offer

WITH US!

 renner.org    facebook.com/rickrenner

 youtube.com/rennerministries    instagram.com/rickrrenner

www.ingramcontent.com/pod-product-compliance
Lightning Source LLC
Chambersburg PA
CBHW061301040426
42444CB00010B/2454